STOCKPORT

Wellington Road South a century ago. The Blossoms Hotel can be seen in the distance, and the imposing 230 ft spire of St George's Church behind it.

BRITAIN IN OLD PHOTOGRAPHS

STOCKPORT

CLIFF HAYES

SUTTON PUBLISHING LIMITED

Sutton Publishing Limited
Phoenix Mill · Thrupp · Stroud
Gloucestershire · GL5 2BU

First published 1997

Title page photograph: Underbank Hall (see page 122).

British Library Cataloguing in Publication Data
A catalogue record for this book is available from the British Library.

ISBN 0-7509-1682-6

Typeset in 10/12 Perpetua.
Typesetting and origination by
Sutton Publishing Limited.
Printed in Great Britain by
Ebenezer Baylis, Worcester.

This book is dedicated to Harry Dearden, a craftsman baker, disc jockey extraordinaire, man of facts and figures (Dearden's Diary), radio personality, and a good mate. No one can make 'Penny Hovis' like you Harry, you are sadly missed.

Trams waiting at the end of the line at Hazel Grove ready to return to Stockport, during the Second World War.

Contents

	Introduction	7
	Acknowledgements	10
1.	Stockport Streets	11
2.	The Churches	41
3.	Parks & Recreation	49
4.	Transport	63
5.	People & Occasions	77
6.	Around Stockport	87
7.	Stockport Then & Now	105

Edgeley Road, Stockport on an Edwardian postcard of the Grenville Series to which we owe a large debt of gratitude for capturing so much of Stockport's past.

INTRODUCTION

In order to understand Stockport's history, and how the town developed, it is necessary to understand the geography of the area. Think of a lovely green valley, a wide 'V' shape, sharper on the left, but higher on the right. At the top the red sandstone has broken through and stands out. Looking up the valley the river running along the bottom of the 'V' splits, and can be traced left and right into the hills at the valley's head. What a lovely tranquil picture we paint, and there you have ancient Stockport.

Man has always had this urge to wander, and when he comes to water, instead of settling down or turning round to go home, he has this urge to cross it. Crossing it could take time, so these crossings were natural sites for dwellings to spring up.

Keeping an eye on who was crossing, and perhaps charging them for the privilege of crossing, was important, and we are reasonably sure that the Romans had, if not a fort, certainly a way-station controlling this border crossing. Mersey means boundary, and this water, now under Stockport, has not only formed the Lancashire–Cheshire border, but in earlier times the Northumbria–Mercia divide.

Saxon times saw quite a settlement, keeping check on travellers crossing the well-established ford at the bottom of Lancashire Hill. This way into Stockport was originally the only one, and the original settlement was where Bridge Street is now. Steps were probably cut into the steep hill up to the Market Place, and maybe even caves for dwellings. A wooden stockade was built at the top, with a place for worship a little back from the edge. Behind this there would have been a clearing for cattle and corn.

After the Norman Conquest William the Conqueror's son, Hugh Lupus (Hugh the Wolf), as Earl of Chester, had orders to divide the area into eight Baronies. Stockport was chosen as one, but the question of who was the first Baron de Stokport could start a good argument. I go along with the theory that it was Nicholas de Spencer and have not found much to make me think otherwise. Although Stockport was not mentioned in Domesday Book, Norbury, Bramhall and Cheadle were.

We find reference to the castle as early as 1173 AD when it was written that Geoffrey de Constantine, as agent of the Baron of Chester, defended the castle at Stokeport against his father Henry II. The wooden fortifications had been replaced by stone before the end of the thirteenth century, and by 1360 the first Lancashire Bridge had been built.

A drawing of Stockport by W. Orme, 1797.

However, during the Civil War, the castle was cleared away by the good citizens of Stockport who reasoned that if they did not have a stronghold or fortified place in the town, then neither side would move in on them. That meant they could not be held in siege or be starved out or taken as hostages. In 1642 they signed the 'Articles of Pacification' in an attempt to stay out of the approaching Civil War. Of course, we know that none of these measures worked, and in May 1644 over 3,000 Parliamentarian troops, under Colonel Dukinfield, waited to stop Prince Rupert of the Rhine and his army from crossing into Lancashire and over to Laythom House to relieve poor Lady Derby. However, the fact that by the time 'Rupert the Fast' arrived in Stopwash (as it was then charmingly known) on 22 May 1644 there were not many Roundheads to be seen in the town, and the fact that only one soldier was actually killed in the Civil War at Stopwash go a long way to vindicate those peace-loving citizens.

You can still see one or two bits of the castle at the back of Great Underbank. In 1775 when Castle Mill was being built for Sir George Warren, and during the excavations for the Muslin Mill, parts of the castle wall and foundations were unearthed, and recorded by local historians.

A charter was granted in about 1225 to Sir Robert de Stokeport to make the town a free borough, and in 1260 it was Prince Edward himself, as Earl of Chester, who granted a weekly market and annual fair to the de Spencers. The family of the de Spencers did not enjoy their position for long however. They chose the wrong side in the uprising led by Simon de Montfort in 1265 and had all their rights and land taken from them and given to the family who took their name from the town, the de Stockports. The last Sir Robert de Stockport died in 1292 and the town passed to his daughter's husband, and then on through other female family members until it ended up with the Warren family, who held the Barony of Stockport from 1370 until Sir George Warren died in 1801. His daughter Elizabeth passed Stockport over to her husband, Viscount Bulkeley of Beaumaris, Anglesey, on the understanding that he change his name to Warren Bulkeley. For such a prize he did, but they had no sons, so the title and land went sideways to Frances Maria Warren whose husband, Lord Vernon of Sudbury Hall, Derbyshire promptly took control. In 1826 it passed to his son, George Warren 5th Baron Vernon, who held it until he sold the manorial rights to the Corporation for £22,500 in 1947. He also sold at auction the Warren estates, the Lord of the Manor's rights to the church (for example, appointing the vicars) and chief rents for the not inconsiderable sum of £120,000, and went off a rich man. He did leave the town one or two gifts though; Vernon Park was one.

In 1835, under the Municipal Corporations Act, Stockport became a borough and the new town council started to straighten up the town, widening and surfacing the roads and reinforcing the bridges. They applied for an Act of Parliament to buy the manorial rights, but it was not until July 1947 that the Act was passed and the completion and paperwork of the sale took place a few years after that. Before 1832 the town was a Cheshire borough and, as the name suggests, Lancashire Hill was in another county. Cheadle Bulkeley (Edgeley) was added, and since the town council took control Heaton Norris, Portwood and Reddish have been incorporated, making up the Stockport area. Stockport became a County Borough in 1889. Offerton was added in April 1935 from the Hazel Grove and Bramhall UDC. The year 1973 saw the emergence of the Greater Manchester County and the unwieldy title of Metropolitan District 12H was given to the lumping together of Stockport, Bredbury & Romily, Marple, Hazel Grove and Bramhall. This was later renamed Stockport MBC.

This short history presents some of the people and names of Stockport's past and puts in context some of the queries that the casual enquirer may have, even if only about the origins of pub names, e.g. Vernon Park – Lord George Vernon; Warren Street – the Warren family (Sir George); Bulkeley Arms – Viscount Bulkeley of Beaumaris.

ACKNOWLEDGEMENTS

Thanks must go to Gordon Coltas (Locofotos) for permission to use all the steam train photographs in this book. Thanks also to Ted Gray for his tram and bus pictures, and to Ann Hurst for her Stockport parks cards and other help. Some cards come from the collection of the Manchester Transport Museum Society, in Heaton Park, and I thank it also. Its restored trams running on a line in Heaton Park, Manchester are well worth a visit for the joy of riding the old-fashioned trams again.

All the new photographs in the section Stockport Then & Now are by Barry Armstrong, photographer, Manchester, and I would like to thank him for allowing me to use them in this book, as well as his patience as I dragged him round Stockport all Sunday morning on more than one occasion. He even put up with being dragged into the odd pub, purely for historical research of course. Thanks also to Jed McCann of Audenshaw, and Bill Newton of Stretford Library for their help. The *Stockport Express & Advertiser* have been most helpful and have given permission for some of their photographs to be used. I would like to thank them and especially Andrew Fraser. I must mention Jim McDermott, boss and driving force of Finchmark Graphics at Bredbury, who gave me the job of calling on every firm in Stockport to try to sell them deskpads. I discovered Higher Hillgate, Lower Hillgate and every ginnel at the back of Stockport, I learnt a new meaning to the words 'Just up the hill', and sold Oxford Blue deskpads to half of Stockport, but I got to know the place. Thanks Jim.

SECTION ONE

STOCKPORT STREETS

Market Place, Stockport, site of the original castle, looking from Petersgate. The Square has been the site of the market since the clearance of the stone remains of the castle and there are references to market traders using the surviving rooms and dungeon to store goods. The postcard was unposted but it is an Edwardian one from about 1908. The pillared building on the left is the original Market Hall (later a hen market) begun in 1850 and built in Yorkshire stone. The balcony was used for election speeches and important public announcements.

Bridge Street, Stockport, *c.* 1905. Looking up Bridge Street from the corner of what was then Heaton Lane, later Prince's Street. The Red Lion on the right of the picture gives the exact location as it is only the side you can see; the front was 1 Heaton Lane and was demolished in 1931. The Red Lion was first mentioned in 1780. In 1817 it was used to quiz prisoners taken during the riots, and in the 1820s it rivalled the White Lion for a long time as a posting station. This postcard shows how built-up the area really was. Somewhere in there is Lancashire Bridge; the photographer was standing in Lancashire, at the bottom of Tiviot Dale, to take this picture.

Bridge Street again, just back from the opposite picture but nearly fifteen years later, *c.* 1920. Prince's Street is to the left, though it is still hard to make out where the bridge itself is.

The other end of Bridge Street, looking towards Market Place, *c.* 1904. At one time this street was known as Briarly's Brow.

Tram passing Tiviot Corner, 1930s. Some parts of Stockport have looked more or less the same for 500 years. This area was decimated when Tiviot Dale station was demolished. The whole area changed, and it needs a little imagination to get it back into context. Lancashire Hill ran down from Chimney Hall and then became Bridge Street over the bridge. The bit of Lancashire Hill from Tiviot Dale to Bridge Street adopted the name Tiviot Dale after the railway station opened. Today, Knightsbridge (where did they get that name from?) replaced Tiviot Dale, and under it runs the River Mersey.

Tiviot Dale looking towards Stockport, *c.* 1905. The early open-topped tram is heading out of Stockport. The hills and slopes presented some problems and there were two runaway accidents here before the 'Westinghouse' braking system was perfected. The chapel on the left can still be seen today.

At last a picture of the bridge itself. Although the original caption on this locally printed postcard says 'Lancashire Bridge' it shows Bridge Street, looking the opposite way from the picture above.

Underbank, Stockport, *c.* 1907. Although the caption says Underbank, the area shown was Little Underbank. The photograph is taken from Great Underbank, probably near the White Lion public house door. The name Underbank first appeared on a map as early as 1454. St Petersgate Bridge, which passes over Little Underbank, was begun in 1866. The clearance work and building-up of the roadway took nearly two years to complete. It cost £10,500 to build, and finally opened to the public on 24 February 1868. At the time it was one of the 'wonders' of the area, being a street over a street, and it bears the coat of arms of Stockport Borough as granted in 1830. The bridge was designed by Mr R. Rawlinson, but today this marvellous piece of engineering is mostly overlooked as the brick approaches are hidden within the buildings on either side, and we tend to regard the bridge as being just the cast iron bit in the middle.

Little Underbank over a century ago. This picture is of the other side of Petersgate Bridge looking back at it. The clock sticking out is on Winter's the Clockmakers and the Albion Hotel is on the corner of Little Underbank and Meal House Brow, which goes off to the right. There once was a meal and cheese house here. The brow seems to have begun a life as a winding brow and later became Dungeon Brow (again a reference to the castle). The dungeon doorway can still be seen on the left on the way up, and was used as a town lock-up around 1800. The last time a man was hung and then displayed on the gibbet at the crossroads at Great Moor as a deterrent to others was in about 1821.

The name Albion is the old name for England and the hotel was given this name as a patriotic gesture in about 1830; before that it was known as the Rising Sun. There had been a hostelry on this site since about 1784. The Albion closed in 1961 and was later demolished. Cannon's Jewellers opened on the site. One previous landlord was Isaac Williamson, a keen botanist, who had a private museum here; many Botanist Society meetings were held here in the late nineteenth century.

Looking up Little Underbank, *c.* 1910. This Grenville postcard is a popular view of Stockport. Walmsley's shoe shop can be seen on the left, and William Fish's hosiery shop on the right. The clock outside Winter's clock shop, which can be seen in the centre of the picture, must be almost as famous as the clock in the centre of Chester.

It is almost a surprise to come across this stairway leading up from Little Underbank to St Petersgate. There is a set of stairs on each side of the bridge, showing how much work went into building it, although most of it is now hidden by the buildings on either side of the cast-iron central section.

If the photographer of the view opposite (top) had turned to the left, this is what he would have seen. The rebuilt White Lion (1904) is on the left, looking down Great Underbank, and G. Wright & Son Dyeing & Cleaning was next to C. & M. Walmsley's shoe shop.

Further down Great Underbank (though the original caption only says Underbank) almost to Bridge Street, and a very early card, sent 6 December 1902. Our writer had to use the front for the message, because only the address was permitted on the back, and she summed up the history and view in eighteen words: 'This is one of the principal streets in Stockport. Some of the buildings are hundreds of years old.'

Bridge Street, 1920. The tram nearest the camera is not a Stockport tram so can be excused for the advertisement on the front. It is a Hyde tram (No. 1) heading home. The one behind with the white top is a Stockport tram. The buildings on the very right of the picture, next to Walters' tobacco and cigar shop is the pub, the Buck and Dog. Although the pub was first mentioned in 1770, this building dates from about 1890. When Lancashire Bridge was widened, both this pub and the Warren Bulkeley were rebuilt. The landlord of the Buck and Dog, James Brown, had a stone set into a corner to mark the height of a flood on 3 August 1779. That same flood also washed away an old bridge at Portwood (Bridge Road). The whole area was under water again in November 1886 when the river rose even higher. One flood every hundred years – I wonder when the next one is due? The pub disappeared, like so much of the area, when the motorway arrived.

A Valentine card from the late 1950s showing Prince's Street just before the revamp of the area that brought in Merseyway. Dewhurst, New Day furniture shop, Boots, Ellis Sykes & Son (fireplaces), Harrisons Sports (including their Boy Scout & Girl Guide department), W. Harvey (saddlers), Ryans (for gowns) – all were there somewhere on the picture, one of a very good series of views that the company produced in their thousands right through the 1960s.

Just two of the many busy firms on Prince's Street. (From the *Stockport Advertiser Year Book 1955* with their kind permission)

Stockport has had two major revamps to its town centre this century. The first was in the mid-1930s and the second in the mid-1960s. The above photograph, taken from the Stockport newspaper, shows work starting on Lancashire Bridge.

Another picture from the local newspaper, taken I think from the viaduct in 1922. It shows very clearly the River Mersey winding its way through Stockport which is well worth a long and careful study. Prince's Street runs almost from top to bottom on the left, and you can make out three trams in the street. Lancashire Bridge, at the top of the picture, has been widened and you can see the foot of the bridge crossing from Hatton Street. The large building at the bottom is the fire station in the corner of Mersey Square, and behind that are the tram sheds for Stockport Corporation Electric Trams. Not much is left of this scene today.

Kingston Mill on Chestergate, once outside the town centre, was, by 1935, surrounded by shops and houses, and was in the way of further developments. This picture, from the local *Stockport Advertiser*, shows the clearing away of the mill as part of the 1930s modernization of the town. Again you can see the footbridge that was very much needed before Merseyway was constructed, and the roofs in the left foreground are the tram sheds. You can still see the plaque that was put up after the redevelopment was completed, on the bridge as you walk under Wellington Road South to the bus station.

Cotton mills were a big part of life in Stockport, even in this century. In 1914 there were sixty-seven cotton firms and 2½ million spindles at work. After the First World War there was a boom in production, but soon many firms were in trouble and not paying dividends. Two large corporations emerged and swallowed up many of the smaller companies. As early as 1900, the Fine Spinners & Doublers Association Ltd had started to take over some of the smaller firms. By 1910 they had acquired the mills of S. Moorhouse, Gorsey Bank, Wear & Brinksway, and many others. The Houldsworth Mill at Reddish (below) was built in 1863 but taken over by the Fine Spinners & Doublers Association Ltd in about 1900.

The mill of Kingston Mill Company (above) was taken over by the second largest company, the Lancashire Cotton Corporation, in the mid-1920s. It was a depressing time with many lay-offs and cut-backs, but the one thing that has been on Stockport's side during times of recession is that it has always had more than one string to its bow. When silk production declined, woollen mills came in, and when they cut back, cotton output rose. Hatting and its associate trades were longstanding local industries, but engineering grew as fast as they cut back. Aeroplanes (Avro and Fairey Aviation) were an important part of engineering in the area and buses were also produced. Stockport was the site of the world's first purpose-built diesel engine factory in 1908.

Mersey Square and Wellington Road North according to the caption, but Mersey Square was just the part on the far side of Mersey Bridge. In the foreground an open-topped Hyde tram crosses what was once called Carr Green, the site of Stockport Fair, which was held on St Mary's Assumption (15 August). Wellington Road North climbs away on the left of the picture and the spire of Christ Church can be seen on the skyline.

The fire station in Mersey Square, *c.* 1920. The station opened on 10 April 1902 and at that time also housed the town's ambulance. A tram is leaving the Corporation Tram Depot and passing the side of the fire station. A couple of drivers going on duty cross the square.

Mersey Square, 1938. The bridge has been widened to cover the river up to Wellington Road South. The North Western bus shelter is still there on the left and the fire station on the far right of the picture.

After the revamp the name Mersey Square crept over to the Cheshire side of the river and the caption on this Grenville card just says Mersey Square, when in fact it shows the Wellington Road South bridge over the Mersey and the road going under to Daw Bank.

A photograph from the bridge itself of Wellington Road South, showing Merseyway with tramlines and Belisha beacons helping pedestrians to get across the large open area, probably late 1940s. The Mersey Hotel survived the first modernization of the area in the 1930s but did not survive later developments in the swinging sixties.

The hilliness of the Market Place area made it difficult for any transport to use this part of town, and because the old centre of Stockport and Underbank was congested, traffic to and from Stockport naturally moved over to Mersey Square. From the 1920s the square became more important for the interchange of transport and once Tiviot Dale station had gone, the transition was completed.

Wellington Road South, looking back into the Mersey Square area, 1939. The corner of the fire station is just visible on the right. The no. 58 tram has made its way from St Petersgate and is about to tackle Wellington Road North before heading out to Reddish. A friendly policeman waits to see you across the road safely.

Wellington Road North (nearer the camera) and Wellington Road South, 1945. The tram, side on, is turning into Mersey Square, and again we have our friendly constable on point duty.

Stockholm Road, looking north towards the 'Monkey Bridge', 1960s. This is the most northerly of the bridges on Stockholm Road crossing the railway lines. The gates on the right of the picture lead to Edgeley Junction sidings and the houses in the distance are in that group of unusually named roads – Moscow, Berlin, Petersburg, and even Finland Road. The church spire in the distance is St Matthew's Church, Edgeley, and you can also just make out the floodlights from Stockport football ground.

St Petersgate and St Peter's Square, 1930s. The names of the streets in this area take a little understanding. The name of the brow that comes up from Mersey Square today was once called Rock Row. Later maps show it marked as Daw Bank, then St Peter's Square, though we know that name should only apply to the small street at the side of the Brick Church.

This picture comes from a brochure for Garner & Sons, House and Land Agents, who had their offices in the Prudential building on the right. In the centre of the picture you can just make out the canopy of the Theatre Royal, built in 1888. The theatre entertained the people of Stockport until it was demolished in 1962. The Abbey National building occupies the site today. The Cobden statue is hidden behind the tram. Richard Cobden was a courageous fighter against the corrupt Corn Laws and was MP for Stockport 1841–7. The statue was unveiled by his daughter Miss Jane Cobden, 27 November 1886.

Another view of St Peter's Square with St Petersgate on the right. The Cobden statue is again hidden behind the tram. Cobden, for the Liberals, was elected along with Henry Marsland in 1841. He was very popular in the town, and did his job well, but at the General Election on 31 July 1847 he stood for Stockport and also for the West Riding of Yorkshire. He polled 642 votes in Stockport and won the seat easily. The Corn Laws had recently been repealed and he was at the height of his popularity. In second place was the Conservative James Healed with 570 votes, and this level of support for his rival may have upset Richard. West Riding was the largest constituency in England and had much prestige, so Cobden decided to take the seat for Yorkshire. Although the people of Stockport pleaded with him, it ended with a re-vote on 16 December 1847 when Liberal James Kershaw got 545 votes and the seat. Cobden was so popular it was even mooted he might stand for both and have two votes; that would have set a precedent, but the rules were not changed and Cobden severed his connection with the town.

When Richard Cobden died on 2 April 1865, the bells of the churches in Stockport had rags wrapped around the clappers, and a dull mournful peal rang out for days. They say that under the statue, a bronze by G. Adams, are a set of coins from 1886, local newspapers, and even a portrait of Stockport's mayor, Joseph Leigh, encased in a time capsule.

The statue was moved in 1965 along with its granite base to its present position on the other corner of the square.

This fine building was the general post office on St Petersgate, *c.* 1906. The dome of the library can be seen in the background. The gantry of telephone lines on the roof of the post office building indicate that that technology was still in its infancy. When telephones were first installed, each line had to have its own wire and insulators, which meant that business premises sprouted these strange-looking contraptions bristling with telephone lines.

The post office opening times were from early in the morning until 10 p.m., seven days a week. You could post letters up to 9.45 p.m. and they were guaranteed to be delivered the next day. Some mail for London posted as late as 11.15 p.m. was taken to Stockport station and sorted on the night mail trains.

Stockport Infirmary, 1904. The infirmary opened on Wellington Road South in 1834, replacing the old 'Dispensary & House of Recovery' in Daw Bank. The old dispensary had to move when Wellington Road was built as part of the Manchester to Buxton toll-pike road. Lady Vernon donated the site for the new infirmary and the foundation stone was laid on 18 June 1832.

The infirmary was completed in October 1833 but had to wait until 20 February 1834 for the transfer of patients from the old dispensary. Built in the classical revivalist style, it was the generous donations and fund-raising dances that paid for the building and even local farmers sent in items for the yearly produce sale to raise more funds. This picture dates from about 1890; it was not until about 1901 that lines were put up for electric trams.

Memorial Hall and Art Gallery. When we think of a war memorial we usually think of some sort of obelisk, or a suitably sad-looking statue, but Stockport wanted something more practical, and what a wonderful memorial they built to those who gave their lives for their country. It is a Memorial Hall and Art Gallery with rooms for exhibitions and was handed over to the Stockport authorities, free from all debt. Built on the site of the old grammar school, on land given by Sir Samuel Kay JP, it cost £24,000, raised 'entirely from public subscription from all classes of persons'. It was started on 15 September 1923 when the mayor, Alderman Charles Royle, laid the foundation stone, complete with its time capsule underneath. Halliday, Paterson & Agate were the builders, and it was opened by Prince Henry, Duke of Gloucester on 15 October 1925. Built in Greek style using Portland stone, it has twenty-three steps up to the classical portico entrance, and you cannot fail to be impressed by the statues, the marble floor and glass roof of the Hall of Memory. Over 2,200 local men gave their lives in the First World War and this was their memorial. Another 780 names of service personnel and civilians killed in the Second World War were added later.

Stockport Town Hall, *c.* 1920. It was nicknamed the Wedding Cake Hall because of the obvious likeness of the tower to the tiers of a wedding cake. This aerial view shows the grand size of the building; at the rear is the apex roof of the wonderful ballroom and concert hall.

Stockport Town Hall, 1911. Before 1904 the Corporation had departments all over the town, and from the turn of the century it had been determined to have a town hall that reflected its high standing and importance. In 1904 it was agreed that the design entered by Sir Arthur Brumwell Thomas be adopted, and the foundation stone was laid in October that year. As one councillor put it, 'even if you go through Stockport by train you won't miss seeing our wonderful town hall, and know how determined we are that Stockport be known throughout the Empire.' The tram passing the hall is Stockport Corporation No. 16, heading for Hazel Grove. Originally built in 1902 with an open top, this tram had been rebuilt in 1912 with a covered balcony, standard staircase and a Dick Kerr K3 body.

Stockport Town Hall, from Wellington Road, just after the Second World War. The town hall was built at a cost of £56,881 by local building contractor Josiah Briggs. It has a frontage of 230 ft facing Wellington Road South, and the main building is 45 ft high. The tower rises 130 ft, but do not expect to hear the sound of bells from the four-faced clock as these were not installed because the building was opposite the infirmary and it was decided that clock chimes or bells would disturb the patients. Prince George, later George V, and his wife, Princess Mary of Teck, opened the town hall officially on Tuesday 7 July 1908. On arrival at the town hall the Prince of Wales was presented with an 18-carat gold key by the designer Sir Arthur Brumwell Thomas. They walked into the main assembly hall with the rest of the royal party which included the Duke and Duchess of Westminster, the Duchess of Buckingham, the Duchess of Chandros and Portland and Viscount Crichton, and before 1,500 invited guests declared the town hall officially opened. Part of Heaton Lane by the Tiviot Dale railway station was renamed Prince's Street in honour of the occasion. As the prince's carriage passed by, a string was pulled and the new street sign fell into place.

The steps behind the tram on the right were to Mount Tabor, a very large magnificent Methodist New Connection Chapel, built in 1866 and demolished in 1969.

This 1946 picture shows the River Mersey flowing under the road and railway bridge at Stockport. The viaduct is really two brick viaducts leaning one against the other. The first crossing was by a goods train on 16 July 1841. A passenger train first crossed on 10 May 1842, and the second viaduct was completed in November 1889; at the time the bridge could handle 200 trains a day.

A postcard from 1950 that merits careful study. It seems to have been taken from the railway viaduct, but the photographer has cut out Wellington Road immediately beneath him. Tiviot Dale Chapel, in the immediate foreground, once nicknamed the 'Cathedral of Methodism', was opened in September 1826 and the last service there was held on 11 July 1971. It was demolished to make way for a smaller, easier to maintain modern chapel a year later. Tiviot Dale station platform can be seen at the bottom right, with what looks like a stone-filled goods train at the platform. Lancashire Hill and its factories, mills, orphanage and churches are middle left, and Portwood with all its crowded mills and factories is on the right. The footbridge over the River Mersey is just discernible – with a magnifying glass.

A general postcard of the glories of Stockport, 1950. The Valentine & Son card was reproduced in thousands and is one of a set taken of the area. Posted in 1952 and sent to Oregon, it found its way back to a postcard fair in Stockport Town Hall. Not unusually this combination card has pictures spreading over ten years. The middle photograph actually has trams in it which had finished running some years before, and the top right picture shows Merseyway cleared of all tramlines and overhead wires.

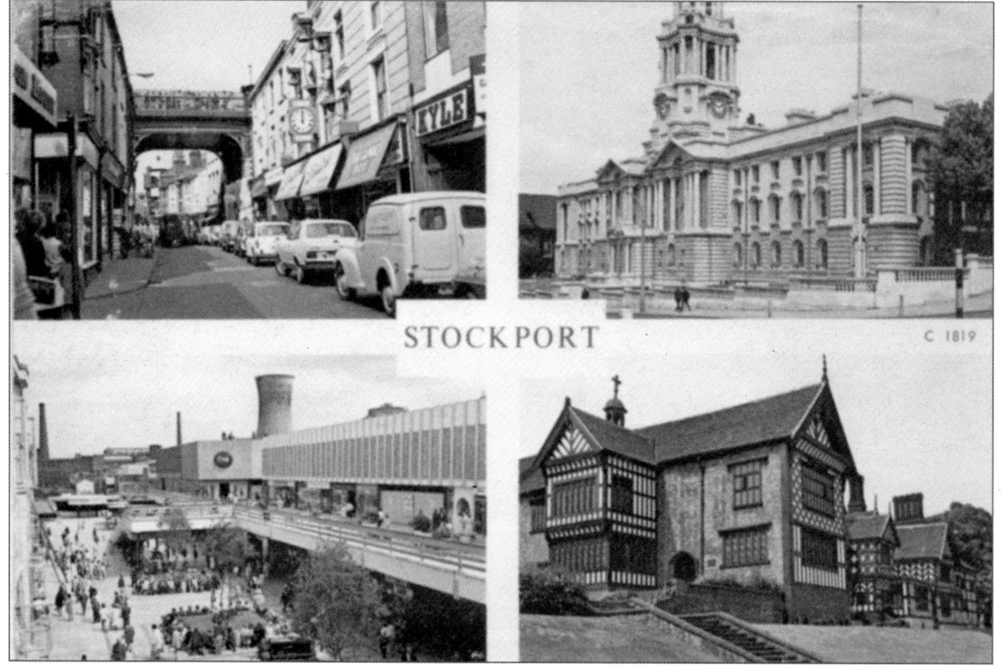

A Judges card, 1970. Now twenty-seven years ago, it seems only yesterday. The picture shows the newly completed Merseyway shopping precinct and Bramall Hall, and below the more traditional views of Little Underbank and the Town Hall.

SECTION TWO

THE CHURCHES

The parish church of Stockport is dedicated to St Mary, but was originally dedicated to All Saints. There has been a place of worship on this site since before Norman times. The earliest part of the church today is in the chancel and dates back to 1190. In 1810 a rebuilding programme for the church began, which lasted about twenty-five years. The story is that when Nelson won the Battle of Trafalgar in 1805 the people of Stockport rang the church bells continuously for a week and put in so much effort that cracks appeared in the church tower. When the bells were rung on 3 October 1809 for King George III they had already put wooden beams in to support the tower and the whole church was in a very bad way.

St Mary's in fine order, 1932. Go today on market days and the whole area around the church is busy, a scene that has changed little over the centuries. A hundred years ago would have seen the verger charging for setting up a stall on the church wall, selling tea to the visiting gentry and getting involved with the bustle of the market. In 1715, charges at the church were: christening and churching 4*d* (churching was the purification and blessing of a mother after childbirth), marriage by publications of banns 1*s* 8*d*, marriage by special licence 5*s*, burial in the churchyard 5*d* adult, 2*d* child, burial in the chancel 6*s* 8*d* (only for the rich).

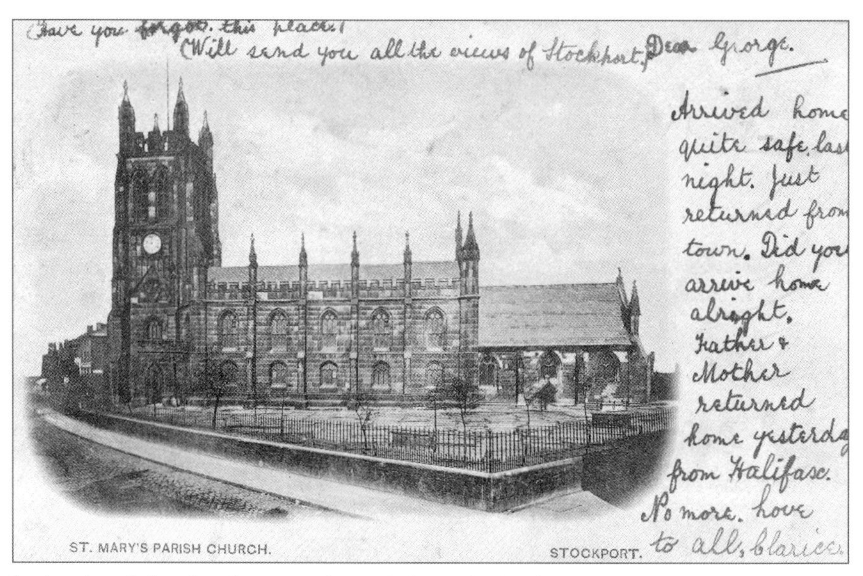

St Mary's Church and churchyard, 1903. The road alongside the churchyard was widened in 1822, and many bodies buried in that part of the churchyard had to be reburied. It was then that this wall with the iron railings on top was built. The bells from 1817 still ring out from their tower today, and the church is a good place to visit for a history lesson. There are memorials to Richard Vernon, windows to Mr L.J. Jennings, MP for Stockport, and of course John Wainwright who wrote the tune 'Stockport' to which John Byrom's *Christians Awake* is sung.

This card shows the Roman Catholic Church of Our Lady and the Apostles in Shaw Heath, 1929. The church is situated just by Greek Street roundabout. It was built in 1905 at a cost of £12,500 and was the principal Roman Catholic church in Stockport. This lovely church spent most of last winter (1996–7) wrapped in scaffolding and plastic sheeting, undergoing renovations.

During the Reformation, Stockport seems to have been a very tolerant town. There are no records of any witch hunts, or priests being persecuted in this area. At the end of the 1790s Catholics could meet and worship if they were discreet. Records from 1803, while not naming the Catholic churches, just record that meetings and services had taken place in Stockport. In the early 1800s Irish immigrants began to settle in Stockport, attracted by the promise of jobs, and by the middle of the century there were approximately 8,000 of them, working in the mills all over Stockport. Then came the cut-backs, and lay-offs, and with them unease and riots. All Catholic processions had been banned but Stockport's RC Scholars went ahead. History records that the Stockport riots started after a session of drinking in an ale house. The pub is called the Gladstone now, but at the time it was the Bishop Blaize (patron saint of wool workers). During the riots St Peter's Church had its windows smashed and St Michael's Roman Catholic Church on St Petersgate was ransacked. The Riot Act was read and troops were sent for from Manchester to quell the rioters. The Mayor of Stockport was later knighted for his handling of the situation.

Stockport Sunday schools annual procession, Wellington Road, *c.* 1913. The Romans had a festival called Terminalia when important people marked their territories with posts and decorated them with flowers. Officials visited the extremes of their territories and dressed trees with ribbons, and there was much ribaldry and merry-making. This pagan festival was brought into the Christian calendar as the Beating of the Bounds when a church would mark its own boundaries with a ceremony. That in turn combined with the walks of witness that take place in Whit Week, when every church and chapel would have a Procession of Witness around its boundaries. People were honoured to take part in the Whit Walks, and if you did not walk, you certainly went and watched. By 1913 it was estimated that about 4,000 people took part in these walks. Whit Walks still take place in Manchester and the surrounding area.

Stockport Sunday School building, just off Wellington Street, 1908. The tall square part was the original school building, started in 1805, and the smaller building with the apex roof nearer the road was the centenary extension, begun in 1905 and opened in 1909. The school itself had begun in about 1785. It had Methodist connections, although it was classed as non-denominational. It began in some cottages down by the river, and grew and grew, until it was claimed to be the biggest Sunday school in the world. By the turn of the century it was generally estimated to have around 4,000 pupils and part-time volunteer teachers, with another 1,000 in its four 'Mission' outposts or annexe schools. One of the men who helped found this remarkable Sunday School movement was called Matthew Mayer, a Wesleyan, converted by John Wesley himself. Mayer did much to help the growth of Wesleyanism in the town and built houses in which the church workers could hold services. The Revd James MacDonald, the second Wesleyan minister of Stockport, lived in one of these houses, earning the curious nickname, 'The Father of the Mothers'. He had one son and four daughters. Each of the daughters married someone famous, and each had a son who excelled in something. One was the mother of Rudyard Kipling. One married Sir Edward Burne Jones (the painter), another married Sir Edward Pointer (painter) and the youngest was the mother of Stanley Baldwin, later Prime Minister. MacDonald's son became the president of the Wesleyan Conference, the highest honour and position in the Wesleyan movement. Not bad for one Stockport family.

St George's Church, Heaviley, 1910. This church celebrated its centenary in 1997. The Bishop of Chester led the celebrations, putting this lovely church in the spotlight, where it deservedly belongs.

St George's Church from Bramhall Lane, 1940. A private road, complete with gates, ran alongside. This sandstone mini-cathedral, larger than the parish church, was the cause of much controversy. It was built because the vicar of St Thomas', the Revd Arthur Symonds, was taking the church higher and higher, and it was not to the liking of his parishioners. Heated arguments and even fisticuffs led to a breakaway group asking the Bishop of Chester, Dr Jayner, for permission to found a new church and parish at Heaviley. Major George Fearn, the main financier, called in all his debts in the town. One family went bankrupt because of this. He also borrowed from a fellow 'rebel', Wakefield Christy-Miller, the hat manufacturer. Christy-Miller gave the land for the church.

Interior of St George's Church, 1904. Designed by H. Austin, the church was consecrated on 25 February 1897 by the Bishop of Chester, and policemen were on the gates to keep out the aforementioned Revd Arthur Symonds, who was livid and threatening trouble. The first vicar was Revd John Thorpe, from Ireland, the grandfather of Jeremy Thorpe, former Liberal leader, and also of John Christie-Miller.

Buxton Road, Stockport, *c.* 1912. This postcard is included to demonstrate the size, style and grandeur of St George's Church, towering above Buxton Road. It has ten bells housed in a 230 ft spire, which could call the whole area to attention. According to the *Illustrated London News*, it was 'One of the finest churches in all England'. It certainly has many fine features inside, including a magnificent organ, and carved detail in the choir stalls.

The picture also shows Higher Hillgate coming in from the left and the Blossoms Inn on the right. The whole area was once called Blossom Hill, only losing the name when Wellington Road opened, 3 July 1826. The official opening procession for the road started from this pub which was renamed the Wellington Inn; however, it slipped back to its old name within five years. The landlord in 1826, one Mr Ford, provided a 'Cold Collation' for those attending the celebrations. For a while the Hatters' Union met here and people looking for casual work would turn up and see what was available.

SECTION THREE

PARKS & RECREATION

Parks were the lungs of the crowded Victorian towns and cities. Councillors and aldermen with civic pride fought for these areas of greenery for the working masses. Above is a view of Lower Vernon Park, 1906. The steps in the park are still there today, but the trees have grown somewhat.

When Lord Vernon sold off his manorial rights in 1849 and looked for something to give back to the town, he decided upon an open area called Vernon Park, completed about ten years later. It was laid out and landscaped, providing the locals with a great environment for walking, promenading and socializing; for the younger ones there were swings and slides. The very early postcard above shows the aviary built by the council, and the ornamental pond. Once Lord Vernon had donated the land, Stockport matched it with amenities. The postcard below shows the same scene fifteen years later, *c.* 1920. The trees have grown and the pond has now assumed the title of 'The Lily Pond'. It was still one of the park's main attractions.

Vernon Park. After parks appeared a curious phenomenon arose: young men in their best (monkey) suits would gather every Sunday afternoon during the summer and walk a certain area, path or part of a park. Young ladies would take their friends, sometimes their younger brothers and sisters, even the bassinet (perambulator) and walk the other way. These became known as the 'Monkey Runs' and the one for Stockport from 1880 onwards was definitely by the Aviary at the bottom of Vernon Park.

The above view of The Walk, at the bottom of Vernon Park captures some of the young ladies 'socializing' with their younger brothers and sisters and looking at others doing the same. Below is another glimpse of the lower park, just off New Zealand Road, with the conservatory and pool. This card was sent in February 1908, and the writer complains of thick snow all over the town.

When Lord Vernon gave this 21-acre park to the town, the good MPs of Stockport decided to donate money to build a museum in it 'to educate the minds of the people'. James Kershaw and John Benjamin-Smith, the Liberal MPs for Stockport, donated this building, again 'To the people', and a museum was started, though local folklore says there had been a museum before, in a public house called the Museum Arms. The museum was opened to the public in 1860; the picture above shows the back of the museum in 1912 and describes it as the refreshment rooms. The card below shows the bandstand in the lower park which provided entertainment for music lovers for about a hundred years. There is, I believe, a Millennium bid for money to re-create this area.

Vernon Park was the first ''open area for the people' in Stockport and will always be special. I do not think that enough people from around the Stockport area know of the museum and park. The galleries in the basement of the museum were opened on 13 October 1995 by Councillor Neville Fields. The galleries currently (1997) house an exhibition of old maps and photographs of Stockport. The above view shows the museum in its green setting; below, the conservatories and flower beds, 1912.

At first I thought that the top card was one of those taken 'Just for You', where you applied to the photographer and they sold you copies to send to your friends. They were very popular from the onset of popular cards in the 1920s until 1960 when the 'masses' started to acquire cameras. However the two ladies are just too far away from the camera for one of those. Maybe Charles Wilkinson of Manchester, who produced the card in the early 1920s, wanted to get a folky, gypsy feel. Anyway it is a card that sets you thinking. Below is a view of the duck pond, Vernon Park, 1927. The lovely pond busy with wild birds of all varieties is now a well-tended sunken garden with a carved stone seat with 'VR' on it.

It is in Vernon Park and its neighbour Woodbank Park that it becomes clear just how steep the banking down to the River Goyt is. The river really is a boundary marker and a feature of both parks. Down at the bottom, next to the Swan Pool and Reservoir, is the weir, pictured above on a 1912 postcard – scenic, peaceful and countrified, though a scramble to reach.

Woodbank Memorial Park started life as the home of the Marsden family; the house was built between 1812 and 1814. When Peter Marsden died the place was empty until bought and given to the town 'as a tribute to the men of Stockport who died in The Great War' by Sir Thomas Rowbottom in 1921. It took time to lay out and restore the property, and it was 29 August 1931 before Sir Thomas declared the hall, and the small local museum there, officially open. Woodbank Hall at one time contained reproductions of the Elgin Marbles and a case full of 'Royal Gifts to the town of Stockport', but it is now used as offices for the Museum Services.

Purchased in 1908 and named after the queen of the time, Alexandra Park was nearer to the centre of the town but not as big as the old Vernon Park and certainly not as landscaped (hilly). It was very popular and soon became noted for its recreational facilities. Edgeley Park was either adjacent or an addition to the park and often postcards proclaimed one, only to show the other. Above is a social outing with children in Alexandra Park on a locally produced Grenville card, 1912. Below is another Grenville card, showing the gentlemen enjoying a quiet 'pipe of baccy' on the bench and the youngsters on the pathway. Is that an early 'Stop Me and Buy One' near them?

Edgeley Park, Stockport, 1904. That area of Stockport has three 'Reservoirs', one running right behind the Stockport FC ground. This is probably the middle one of these. The one nearest Alexandra Park has been given the name Sykes Pond and is very clean and well kept, with numerous well-fed ducks and geese on it, and a model boat club that seems to be very popular.

The caption on this Grenville card, posted in 1913, says Park Gates, Edgeley Road, but that is not the whole story. The park is the Alexandra Park, and the street, even though it is Edgeley Road on the A–Z today, still has little markers saying Castle Street.

Edgeley Park, Stockport, 1908. When the park first opened on 1 May 1889 it covered just over an acre of land, but an extension opened on 2 May 1903 made it almost three acres. Alexandra Park came later, opening Easter 1908. Named after the queen, it was considerably larger at just over 10 acres. On the whole Stockport can be very proud of its parks.

Lyme Hall, drawn by P.C. Auld, *c.* 1850. Lyme Hall was the home of the Legh family for 600 years until the end of the Second World War. Lord Newton decided that the upkeep of the estate was too much for the family and gave it to the National Trust, who, though grateful to receive 'such a gift of great importance', knew they had to put into place funding or management to preserve the place, take care of its expensive upkeep and tackle some of the work that urgently needed doing. Various uses were mooted, including a teacher training college or a convalescent home, before the National Trust and Stockport Borough Council agreed in March 1946 that the borough would be granted a 99-year lease on the condition that 'the council would undertake full responsibility for upkeep; to reserve the park as an open space; to agree to the showing of certain rooms in Lyme Hall to the public; and use or sub-let the remainder of the Hall for some purpose to be agreed by the National Trust'.

The donor, Lord Newton was involved in all the discussions, as was the Earl of Crawford and Balcarres, head of the National Trust at the time. The Earl himself later sold his own family seat of Haigh Hall to Wigan Corporation. The Lyme Hall agreement was the first time a local corporation had been allowed to take over one of the National Trust's properties. As soon as it was announced, the council set up a committee which was inundated with requests to use the facilities. The council was surprised at the range of interest shown in Lyme Hall. They had applications from farmers wanting to graze their sheep, from people wanting to use it for horse racing, motorbike scrambling, fishing and youth camps, a group wanting to shoot every rabbit in the park and another who wanted gospel meetings round bonfires.

Caretakers, and special police had to be taken on to keep the place safe when Lord Newton moved out. Park-keepers were added to the council's wages bill to stop people from cutting down trees and even poaching the deer. The Stockport park superintendent had his men make 2,000 new plants out of old stock to start replenishing the Dutch Gardens, and another 1,000 herbaceous plants were put into nursery lines in Woodbank Park ready to move to Lyme in the autumn.

Lord Newton agreed to leave certain items of furniture and the National Trust put in their regional representative Lt. Col. Brocklehurst, who was so valuable in the time up to the opening of the hall, 14 June 1947. HRH the Duchess of Kent agreed to come and perform the opening ceremony. Prestbury sculptor, Alan Brough cut the plaque using local stone called 'Hopton Wood' but at the last minute the Duchess had to fly to Greece to her mother who was very ill and Earl Crawford stepped in on the day. The Duchess did come as soon as she was able and on 18 July the hall was opened for the second time.

Lyme Hall, Cheshire, drawn by T. Allom, 1837. Lyme Hall partly dates from the sixteenth century and is described in *King's England* as 'one of the noblest of Cheshire's Great Houses'. Its recent management has been a success story, and Stockport and the National Trust can be congratulated. It is very well worth a visit.

Visitor numbers to the park and hall have gone up since they made the recent television adaptation of Jane Austen's *Pride and Prejudice* there.

Abney Hall, Cheadle just off Manchester Road, one of Stockport's 'gems'. The picture shows the hall today. The original house is in the centre, and the additions from 1849 are on the extreme left, with further 1893 additions on the right.

Originally the house was called The Grove and was built by Ralph Orrel, a Stockport Cotton Spinner. His son, Alfred Orrell, and Maria, who married in October 1847, were to make it their home, but as the house was not ready for them, they moved into the The Cottage at Grassmere in Westmorland. Unfortunately, Alfred died before the house was completed and it was put up for auction on 15 May 1849. The auctioneer's bill stated that it was 'a mansion of Norman Gothic style, on the turnpike road between Didsbury and Cheadle. Recently laid out by an eminent landscape gardener, and through the grounds a brook flows, with a cascade which can be seen from the front windows.'

James Watts subsequently bought the house. He was a town councillor for Manchester and later became mayor of the city in 1855–7. It was his eminent guests who made this place so special. He changed the name to Abney Hall after Sir Thomas Abney (1640) who was a great 'Dissenter' and friend and benefactor to Dr Watts who wrote so many great hymns, including *Oh God Our Help in Ages Past*. Gladstone and his wife, Disraeli and his wife, and Cobden and Bright were guests, but grandest of all was Prince Albert, who stayed for nearly a week in 1857 while planning the Royal Treasures Exhibition at Old Trafford. He visited again for three days a few years later, arriving with his entourage of dukes, earls and Life Guards. These visits excited the whole area. The smart soldiers posted on the gates and the grounds brought hundreds of sightseers.

No mention of Abney Hall can be made without recalling little Agatha Miller, who, with her widowed mother, spent many Christmases and holidays here after her elder sister Madge married the young James Watts. She is of course better remembered as Agatha Christie, and wrote of her fond memories of the hall in the introduction to *The Affair of the Christmas Pudding*. The Watts family lived in the Hall until 1958, when it passed into the hands of the Cheadle & Gatley UDC and became their council offices. (Shutterspeed)

Luckily, the Bruntwood Group bought Abney Hall from the council and proceeded to restore it to its former glory. Even though Bruntwood have offices in the building, their sympathetic renovations have ensured that everything is in keeping with its original character. Each year on Heritage Day they open the doors to the public. This lovely hall proves eloquently that modern go-ahead offices need not be of concrete and glass; with some care and imagination such lovely old buildings as Abney Hall can still have a use. (Shutterspeed)

Marple Hall, 1950s. A seventeenth-century home built by the Bradshaw family on the remains of a medieval home of the Vernons, Marple Hall will always be associated with John Bradshaw, as 'the home of the man who sentenced a king to death'. Though to be fair there were other signatories on Charles' death warrant, John Bradshaw seems now to be taking most of the blame.

SECTION FOUR

TRANSPORT

Mersey Square, May 1942. Photographs of street life during the war are fairly rare. Taking photographs of streets or buildings was frowned upon and even banned. What makes this picture more interesting is that it shows lady conductresses doing their 'bit' while the men were away. The front tram is from the SHMJ (Stalybridge, Hyde & Mossley Joint Tramway). These trams ran from Stockport to Hyde. They were painted in a green livery, and their local name was the 'green linnets'. The other trams are Stockport Corporation ones.

Stockport Corporation tram car No. 66 leaves Mersey Square on route 35B heading for Manchester. The No. 35 ran to Piccadilly, Manchester, and the No. 35B route ran to Albert Square. Electric trams began a service between Manchester and Stockport in January 1903 and the last through tram finished in 1949, but trams still ran in Stockport right up until 1951.

Mersey Square, Stockport, 1949. A Stockport tram looking past its best trundles back to the depot after a Saturday lunchtime duty taking fans to the Stockport football ground at Edgeley. The trams in their cheerful red and white livery with the Stockport Corporation crest on the side were a very popular sight in the town, and were often used for football specials and even for day outings.

St Peter's Square, Stockport tram terminus, 1921. It had a four-track layout, and this photograph shows a Stockport Corporation tram, No. 60, on the right with the driver and conductor posing for the cameraman. The other tram, No. 125, is an older Manchester one, and is getting ready to return on the 35 route back to Piccadilly, Manchester. (Ted Gray Collection)

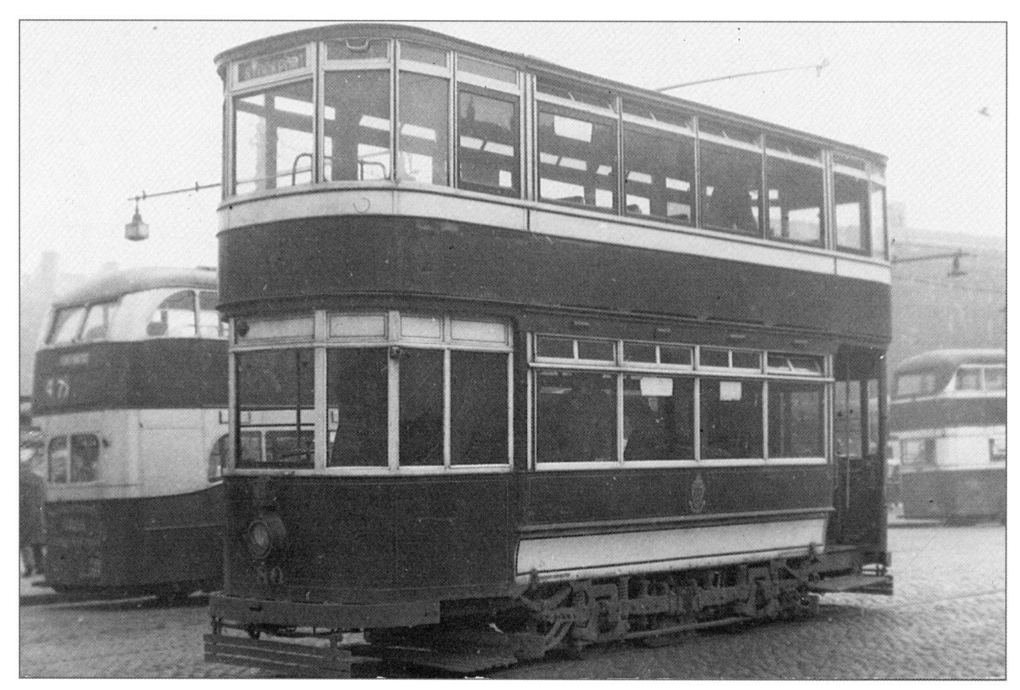

Manchester Piccadilly, *c.* 1948. A Stockport tram stands in Piccadilly Gardens ready for its journey back to Stockport on the 35 route. Apart from on the very early trams, which had general advertisements at each end, Stockport had decided it would not carry advertising on the sides of its trams, and this gave them a very clean and tidy look. A Manchester bus stands to the left of the picture and a SHMD (Stalybridge, Hyde, Mottram & Dukinfield) bus on the right. (W.J. Haynes)

Prince's Street, Stockport, late 1949. After Manchester decided to abandon its trams, Stockport cut back on its tram services, and the Cheadle Heath lines were closed. The tramlines into Mersey Square were also not used and trams terminated in Prince's Street, seen here as drivers and conductors relax at their makeshift depot. (Manchester Transport Museum Society Collection, Heaton Park, Manchester)

Looking down towards Mersey Square, *c*. 1920. This postcard shows Manchester tram car 584 just about to ascend Daw Bank. When this route began, the No. 35 trams were not allowed to carry passengers up the bank as their brakes were not considered good enough. It must have been very frustrating having to get off the tram and watch it head up, empty, to where you wanted to go. The situation lasted some six months until the trams were fitted with Westinghouse Magnetic Track Brakes. The Wellington Road South Bridge and the Stockport Railway Viaduct are both clearly visible on this postcard. The tramlines went through the roadway arches then round and over the arch through which they had just come, heading south. This circular climb was said to be unique to Stockport. Another unusual point was that, although the tramlines were laid up and down St Peter's Square, trams never ran down them and these lines were soon taken up. (Manchester Transport Museum Society Collection)

Stockport tram No. 78 has climbed Lancashire Hill and is heading for Houldsworth Square and Reddish, though its back indicator board has been left at 'Stockport' ready for its return journey. Brakes were a problem for Stockport trams because of the hilly nature of the town centre. There were several accidents in the first months of service. On Tuesday 10 September 1901 a tram became derailed after coming down Lancashire Hill too fast and demolished the front of Horrocks' clog shop. There was another runaway tram down Lancashire Hill on 4 June 1902. Fortunately nobody was seriously hurt in either incident. (Manchester Transport Museum Society Collection)

Heaton Lane, *c*. 1906. The open-top tram dates this postcard to the early years of trams in Stockport, as all the trams were delivered with open tops. When Stockport knew the end of its tram services was inevitable the corporation decided to finish on an historical note. The first electrified Stockport tram was officially inaugurated on Monday 26 August 1901 and the last tram ran on 25 August 1951, fifty years later to the day. Driver Joe Hartington was the driver of the first official tram and he was 'guest' driver and passenger on the last one. The first and last tram also ran over the same section, up Lancashire Hill to Sandy Lane. Since so many people wanted to make that special last journey, three trams had to be used. Service car 82 was full of enthusiasts, reserve car 57 filled up with long-serving members of the corporation transport department and car 53 (illuminated) carried the mayor, members of the town council and other officials. Some of the officials were very worried in case it began to rain, because they thought that the hot bulbs on the illuminated tram would explode, but luckily it didn't. The last tram in service in the Greater Manchester area was greeted on its last journey by cheering crowds, football rattles and majestic splendour.

The Mid-Cheshire Motor Bus Company ran one of the earliest omnibus services from Stockport until they were taken over by the North Western Road Car Company in 1925. They were not the first though; as early as 1908 a Mr Frank Clayton had started a service from the Thatched House pub near the Rectory on Churchgate to the Jolly Sailor, Marple, where he had a garage. It was a double-decker, open-topped bus, and it ran at two-hourly intervals, for a fare of 4*d*. This service finished abruptly in July 1912 because of financial difficulties. (Leyland Motors Ltd)

A 1930s advertisement for the Crosville Motor Company which ran buses to villages all over Cheshire from Stockport. The company was partly owned by the government.

A Stockport Corporation bus, newly delivered from the Leyland Motor Company and in pristine condition ready to go into service. This photograph was probably taken in 1939 just before the outbreak of the Second World War. (Leyland Motors Ltd)

An advertisement for the North Western Road Car Company, 1936. Despite its name, Road Car Company, it ran buses and coaches in the Stockport area.

Mersey Square, Stockport, 1954. The corporation had purchased most of its buses from Leyland Motors in Lancashire, even though there was a bus builder locally. Now and again the corporation did use the local bus company Crossley from Ewood Road in Stockport, and this photograph shows the No. 23 bus, built in 1951 by Crossley for the corporation. The buses continued the tradition of the trams by not carrying advertisements. (Ted Gray)

Ashbridge, Stockport, 1 August 1963. Light engined 'Jubilee' class *Tonga* heads for Edgeley Motive Power Depot in light steam. The sheds at Edgeley (9B was the shed number) were quite important and always contained a number of express and named engines. (Gordon Coltas, Locofotos)

Tiviot Dale station, 4 April 1966. The four lines going through the station were needed as the line was much used by freight trains. These usually went through on the middle lines, keeping out of the way of the 'stoppers' (passenger trains). This is probably why there are not many photographs of Tiviot Dale station compared to Edgeley station with its London expresses. With the George Road goods and shunting yard on the other side of the viaduct, over 75 per cent of trains through Tiviot Dale station were goods trains. Here the unusual Crosti-boilered 92027 heads east with mineral wagons. (Gordon Coltas, Locofotos)

Heaton Chapel station, 22 October 1964. An Up coal train is headed by 42804 through the station, taking the slow line next to the platform. Built in 1962, this 2–6–0 locomotive is showing signs of leaking and wear as the steam age draws to a close. (Gordon Coltas, Locofotos)

Stockport Viaduct, 1 August 1965. 'Black Five' (Mickey) No. 44677 crosses the viaduct with a parcels train. Although electrification of lines had taken place, steam workings were still seen, especially on the less prestigious turns such as parcels and empties. The fact that Stockport Viaduct was built in two parts shows up well in this photograph. (Gordon Coltas, Locofotos)

Heaton Mersey Motive Power Depot locomotive shed code 117E, 2 November 1963. A 'Jubilee' class 45732 *Sanspareil* stands at the coaling depot at Heaton Mersey sheds. You can see the belt and tipper that put the coal straight into the tender of the steam engines. This depot and station were to vanish under piles of soil and rubble after the line closed in 1969. Now houses and industrial units cover what was once a large railway complex. (Gordon Coltas, Locofotos)

Heaton Mersey was a busy spot on the LMS railway. There was a large marshalling yard next to George Road (B&Q today) and it meant that 'Black 8s' (Mickeys) and 'Austerity 90s' were always around. Here 'Jubilee' 45732 *Sanspareil* (named after one of the Rainhill entries) has backed down to buffers and waits under the footbridge ready to go back into the shunting yard. The River Mersey and the railway bridge are in the background. (Gordon Coltas, Locofotos)

Tiviot Dale railway station just before its demolition in June 1968. The station opened on 1 December 1865 and trains ran to Altrincham and on to Liverpool, giving an alternative to going into Manchester. It served Godley, Marple and Woodley the other way. Contrary to popular belief, it was not the 'Beeching Axe' or railway cutbacks that saw the closure of this line, but an accident caused by construction workers who were building the M62. They did so much damage to the tunnel under the A6 that the line could not be used, and in the end it was abandoned. This picture shows the rather ornate face of the station with Tiviot Chapel in the background, and the granite sets in the forecourt.

SECTION FIVE

PEOPLE & OCCASIONS

The Stockport Advertiser *captured the first formal visit to the town of the 1st Battalion of the Cheshire Regiment, 9 October 1954. The Cheshires are pictured here passing the town hall, where Mayor John W. Bennett JP was among those taking the salute.*

Buxton Road and the Davenport cinema, 1938. The cinema contained a posh cafeteria; you can see the CAFÉ sign on top of the façade. The cinema opened in June 1937, in the pre-war flush of entertainment palaces, and very unfortunately closed in March 1997, with a concert including Andy Prior, band leader, and Bill Tarmey (Jack Duckworth in *Coronation Street*). Among the stars who appeared in the annual Davenport pantomime over the years were Les Dawson, Roy Barraclough, John Inman, Lewis Collins, Ken Dodd and many more, too many to mention.

Stockport's steam-powered fire engine in action at Nelstrops Mill, 1893. The number of mills which had sprung up in and around Stockport made a good fire brigade a necessity. The first steam-powered fire engine was purchased in 1870 to replace the old hand-carts. At the time of this picture the fire brigade headquarters were in Corporation Street, but they moved to Mersey Square in 1902, along with their only ambulance. The new station opened on 10 April 1902, and dominated Mersey Square until the second reorganization of the area in the 1960s when it was demolished.

This Edwardian postcard captures day trippers coming off Cheadle Hulme station. One might guess that they had been somewhere exciting, though a police sergeant stands on the platform, to make sure no one misbehaved.

The yard of Bell's Brewery, 1908. The brewery, which was started in about 1836, was in Hempshaw Lane, Stockport, and was one of the leading breweries in the area. In this picture the dray horses are ready with a load of barrels for delivery. The beer at the time was three ha'pence a pint. Bell's Brewery also owned a number of public houses, but in 1949 it was taken over by the larger Robinson's Brewery which for a time used the premises in Hempshaw Lane, before withdrawing everything to its own central offices. The pubs all changed over to Robbie Ales. The Tiviot Dale, The Blossoms, Heaviley and the Adswood, are all former Bell's pubs.

Advertisement for the brewery, 1930s.

The visit of Her Majesty Queen Elizabeth, as part of her Silver Jubilee Celebrations, 21 June 1977. The Queen is seen here leaving the Royal Train at Hazel Grove station to tour the area. Seems like only yesterday but it was twenty years ago!

In the early 1930s a number of police boxes were built in the Stockport area which was one of the first in England to adopt this system. The local press and the leaflets handed out referred to them as 'miniature Police Stations in every detail'. They were built of ferrocrete and reinforced metal, and were about 5 ft square inside. 'A member of the public who desires the police, ambulance or fire brigade can proceed to the nearest box, and by opening the cupboard marked telephone, and lifting the receiver, is automatically connected with headquarters.' There were facilities for writing, storing documents, a first-aid box, and electric light and radiator. In fact 'The box answers all the requirements of modern policing except for accommodation'. These police boxes lasted until just after the war, when more people acquired their own telephones.

CHESHIRE YEAR BOOK. 45

STOCKPORT BOROUGH POLICE FORCE.

TELEPHONE 2002, 2003 and 2010.

Central Station.—Vernon Street.

Sub-Station.—Gorton Road, Reddish.

Chief Constable : Mr. G. W. Robotham. Superintendent and Deputy Chief Constable : Mr. Ernest Southern.

SITUATION OF POLICE BOXES.

(For Police, Fire and Ambulance Emergencies).

Great Portwood Street, corner of Schoolyard, St. Paul's School.
Corner of Graham Road, Offerton Lane (opposite Union Chapel).
Corner of Mile End Lane and Lowndes Lane, nr. Co-operative Stores.
Woodsmoor Lane, near Electric Sub-Station.
Adswood Road, opposite Beech Road.
Adjoining grounds of Union, Shaw Heath, near Holland's Mill.
Corner of Longshut Lane and Higher Hillgate (opposite Shakespeare Hotel).
Middle Hillgate, corner of Edward Street (opposite Waterloo Road).
Corner of Park, Edgeley Road, just below tram terminus on left.
Corner of St. Matthew's Schoolyard, Chatham Street.
Adjoining Lavatory, Cheadle Heath Railway Bridge, Stockport Road, Cheadle Heath.
Corner of Tadswell's Court, Heaton Lane.
Land adjoining Baker Street Mission, Belmont Street.
Manchester Road Electric Sub-Station.
Corner of Wellington Road North and Manchester Road, Heaton Chapel.
Thornfield Road, Heaton Moor, corner of Green Lane, near old Council Offices.
Land in Parsonage Road, opposite Earl Road, Heaton Chapel.
Didsbury Road, opposite Playing Fields, Heaton Mersey.
Corner of Newbridge Lane and Alpine Road.
Corner of Buxton Road and Dialstone Lane.
Didsbury Road, corner of Langham Road.
Broadstone Road, corner of Houldsworth Street.
Tram Terminus, Gorton Road, North Reddish.
Junction of Mill Lane, Windmill Lane and Longford Road.
Corner of Reddish Road and Woodhall Road, South Reddish.

A page from the 1935 yearbook for Stockport showing where these miniature police stations were.

A composite picture of views taken inside the Mirrlees Blackstone Ltd factory at Hazel Grove. Top, the crankshaft machining shop and K.V. engines in the test bay; below, setting the cutting heads and drilling bed plates. Mirrlees started in Glasgow where in 1897 they built the first diesel engine in Britain, in fact in the then British Empire and only the third in the world. As Mirrlees, Bickerton & Day they built the Stepping Hill factory in 1907, the first purpose-built diesel engine factory in the world. In 1936 they employed 2,500 people in their Bramhall Moor Lane factory.

The Coal Strike of 1912 was just one of many strikes by workers fighting for better conditions. Seamen, printers, railway workers and coalminers were always at the cutting edge of trouble, though in 1907 in Stockport, hatters were part of a 'lock-out' by the masters. In this picture, poor people are queueing to buy coal at 1*s* per hundredweight from the coal sidings next to the railway line in Wellington Road South.

Heaton Mersey Red Cross Hospital, *c.* 1908. Each area had its own identity, and everything needed for local existence, including its own town hall.

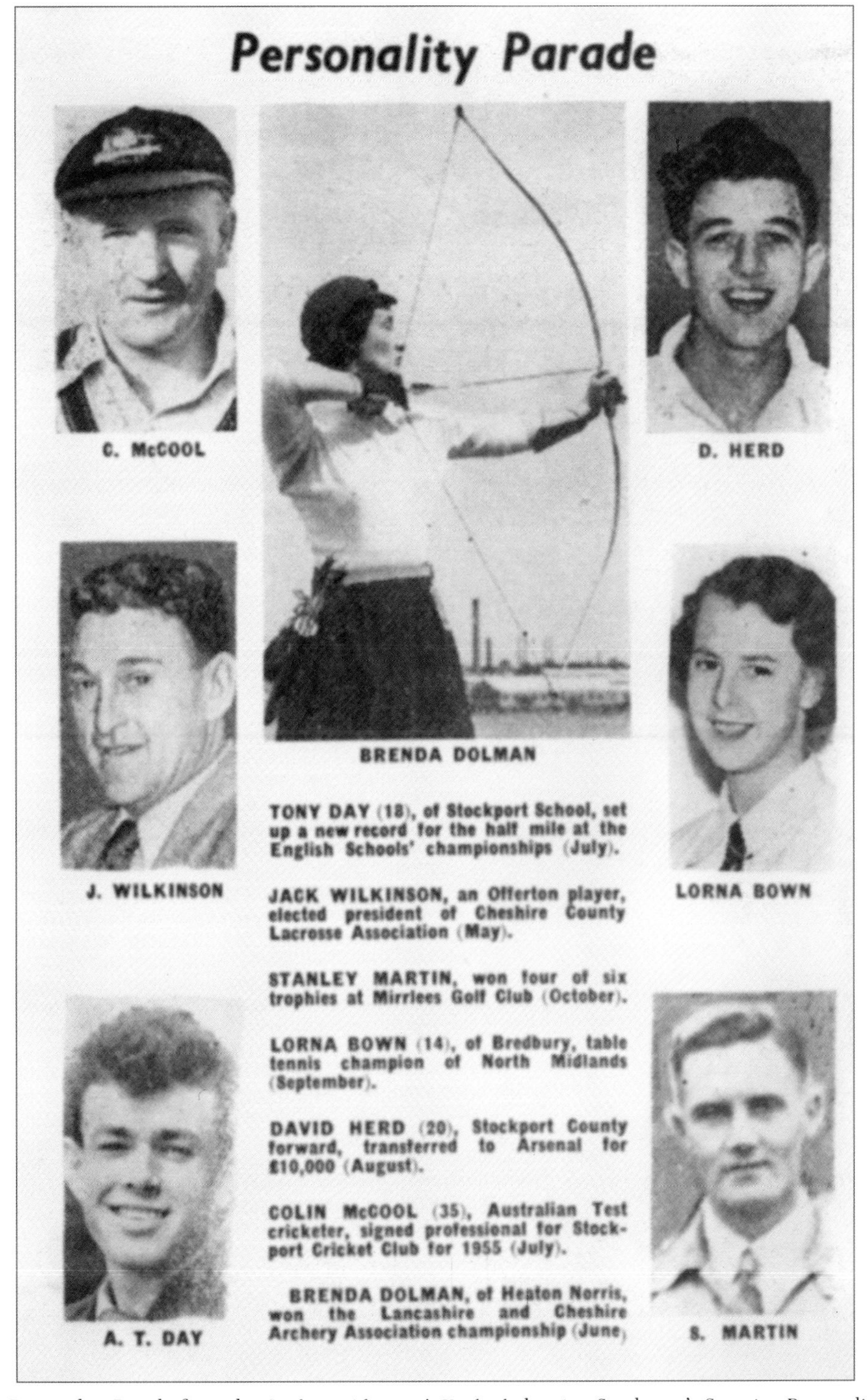

Personality Parade

C. McCOOL

D. HERD

BRENDA DOLMAN

J. WILKINSON

LORNA BOWN

TONY DAY (18), of Stockport School, set up a new record for the half mile at the English Schools' championships (July).

JACK WILKINSON, an Offerton player, elected president of Cheshire County Lacrosse Association (May).

STANLEY MARTIN, won four of six trophies at Mirrlees Golf Club (October).

LORNA BOWN (14), of Bredbury, table tennis champion of North Midlands (September).

DAVID HERD (20), Stockport County forward, transferred to Arsenal for £10,000 (August).

COLIN McCOOL (35), Australian Test cricketer, signed professional for Stockport Cricket Club for 1955 (July).

BRENDA DOLMAN, of Heaton Norris, won the Lancashire and Cheshire Archery Association championship (June)

A. T. DAY

S. MARTIN

The Personality Parade from the *Stockport Advertiser's Yearbook* showing Stockport's Sporting Personalities, 1955. At least one of them became a household name. David Herd was a 'Busby Babe' at Manchester United and played for England. He is still around, running a garage firm in the Urmston area.

The Heaton Mersey lacrosse team, 1955, which drew 10–10 with Old Hulmeians and then won the Senior Flags in the replay by 8–7.

Manchester City footballer Mr Don Revie (right) presents the Table Tennis award to Cheshire players in Stockport, October 1954.

Section Six

Around Stockport

The name Bramhall comes from 'The nook where broom grows'. This postcard shows Bramhall village ninety years ago. The horse-drawn transport has provided plenty of that stuff 'that's good for the roses' lying in the street. A van advertising aerated water is seen making a delivery on the left.

Bramhall village, *c*. 1935. It looks a really calm and quiet village, compared with today's hustle and bustle, yellow lines and 'street furniture'.

This photograph could be as early as 1910, and depicts Bramhall Lane South looking back towards the village centre.

Bramhall Lane, Bramhall, 1918. This picture was taken well down the lane off the Buxton Road.

Bramhall in the 1920s is what this card is supposed to represent, but all five pictures are of parts of Bramall Hall and the grounds. The name of the hall once had an 'h' in it as the village does but Bramhall Hall is awkward to say, so the 'h' was dropped.

Bredbury, Redhouse Lane, *c.* 1912. This picture was taken from the recreation ground and Sidebotham Street. The church in the distance is St Mark's.

Bredbury, 'the stronghold built on planks of wood', 1930. Not much of that is showing here on this postcard of Bents Lane, looking up towards Stockport Road, East and West.

Cheadle Green, 1933 – a photograph by W. Marsh from a 'Come and Live in Lovely Cheadle' brochure produced just before the Second World War. Mr Marsh was standing in the side drive of Abney Hall, which was where Agatha Christie finally ended up when, after 'disappearing', she was 'discovered' in Harrogate. She recorded that she used to walk to the church every Sunday when resting at Abney, so she would have walked through the Green.

Cheadle, 1937. Cheadle is in Cheshire and no amount of boundary changes will ever alter that. This postcard was specially printed for S. Briscall, who might have been the landlord of the George & Dragon Hotel. The pub and the bank on the corner are still there.

High Street, Cheadle, with Ashfield Road on the right, 1932. The bank and hotel are in the middle of the picture. Cheadle is said to mean 'The wood near the water meadow' though it could also mean 'where the wood is' as the ancient name was 'Cedde' (wood) and the 'le' at the end might derive from 'ley', meaning 'wood' in old Norse.

Corner of Gatley Road and Wilmslow Road, Cheadle, *c*. 1910. The easily recognizable Deacon's Buildings on the corner have had quite a few names but they have always been a café. Charles J. Large had a cycle shop below the tea rooms.

Cheadle Heath, *c.* 1907. This view is along Stockport Road towards Stockport, with the Farmer's Arms away on the corner of Edgeley Road. The tram carries an advertisement for 'Sparkla' fizzy drink. Both top and bottom decks were open to the elements and the driver had to continue rain or shine. It was not until 1912 that local trams were enclosed.

Cheadle, showing the Electra Café next to the Electra cinema on Cheadle High Street. The café next to Boots advertised that it was open from 8.30 a.m. until after the film had finished at 10 p.m.

Wellington Road South in either Heaviley or Edgeley, about 100 years ago. The horse-drawn tram dates this photograph, taken from a glass slide, to before 1900. However, back in the mist is the spire of St George's Church, so it must be after 1896. The large hotel on the left is the Nelson, built just before 1830.

Davenport, Bramhall Lane, looking away from the station towards Stockport, with Kennerley Road to the right, 1928. One of the police boxes mentioned on page 82 is just discernible on the pavement in the centre of the picture.

Hazel Grove, and the Rising Sun Inn before it was timbered to make it look older. Buxton Road is on the left; the Macclesfield Road cannot quite be seen to the right of the inn. Under the lamp in the centre is the Jubilee Fountain, put up in 1897 for Queen Victoria's Jubilee, which provided two metal cups for thirsty passers-by. The fountain also has two granite troughs for horses, and four lower troughs for cats and dogs. It cost £173 18*s* 3*d* and was paid for by Mr E. Carver.

Hazel Grove, outside the Rising Sun, *c.* 1945. Two trams wait at the end of the line to return to Stockport.

Bullock Smithy Hotel, *c.* 1900. Hazel Grove was formerly called Bullock Smithy. In 1835 its residents, wanting a better name, voted to change it to Hazel Grove. The site of the hotel is in Torkington Park today. Originally the road ran past the door of the hotel, but was re-routed in 1820 to set the hotel back. The smithy itself was opposite the hotel.

Hazel Grove, London Road, outside the Red Lion Hotel looking south, *c.* 1910. The Red Lion dates back to 1754. The tower of St Thomas', Norbury parish church is behind.

Heaton Chapel, Wellington Road North, near the junction of School Lane, pictured here on a Lilleywhite card, *c.* 1960.

Heaton Chapel, Manchester Old Road, looking towards Stockport, around the turn of the century. Manchester Road leading to Lancashire Hill was once the main road from Manchester to Stockport. When Wellington Road was completed it became a secondary road and, as it was steeper than the new road, remained almost unchanged for over sixty years.

Heaton Chapel, Wellington Road North, looking back towards the Old Toll Bar and the Toll House, *c*. 1904. Manchester Road goes off to the left and Wellington Road to the right down to Stockport. This bit of road in the foreground was called Stockport Road at one time. The local postcard is by T. Everitt Innes.

Heaton Chapel, *c*. 1920. This is the view towards Manchester from the point on Wellington Road North, where the last photographer stood. The corner of the Toll House is just visible on the right.

Heaton Moor Road, Heaton Moor. An Edwardian view of the shops looking back towards Heaton Chapel and the railway station.

Heaton Moor Road, Heaton Moor, and the same shops, but looking the other way on another fine local postcard by T. Everitt Innes. The area only developed when the railway arrived, and Manchester's merchants built houses near the railway station to be among the first commuters, though always first class.

Heaton Norris and Wellington Road, 1920. This is a Grenville postcard.

Heaton Mersey, Didsbury Road, looking from Didsbury towards Stockport. This card is postmarked 1905 but the picture probably dates from earlier than that.

Marple Bridge, *c.* 1938. This is a lovely rural picture showing Brabyn's Brow looking over Marple Bridge. The Norfolk Arms was named after the duke who held lands in the High Peak area. Lower Fold goes off to the left and Town Street to the right. It was the fast-flowing River Goyt which gave impetus to the development of Marple as a textile town.

Marple, Market Street. The postcard dates from 1945, though the picture could be earlier. Market Street was one of the principal shopping streets in the district. It was here in Marple that Samuel Oldknow, renowned for his compassionate attitude to his workers and his innovative schemes for their social welfare, set up his revolutionary factories; not far from this picture is a road named after him.

Hall Street, Offerton, early 1960s. Old Charlie Rum and Hovis with real butter are among the advertisements on the left.

Reddish, Broadstone Road. This picture, looking up towards the railway bridge, was taken before trams arrived.

Gorton Road, Reddish, just after the First World War. The view back towards Stockport down Gorton Road includes a tram returning towards Houldsworth Square.

Reddish Lane and the tram terminal, *c.* 1930. The end of the line as far as Stockport trams were concerned was up Gorton Road to Reddish Lane to the terminus pictured here. Cranbrook Road is on the left with Brook Green cemetery behind it.

Houldsworth Square, Reddish, 1930s. Without the Houldsworth family the village of Reddish would never have been developed. Henry Houldsworth purchased an estate at Reddish near Stockport in 1864 and erected a large mill for cotton spinning. His son William Houldsworth also built mills in Reddish, and through his generosity a thriving village soon emerged. He paid for the schools, the church, and a working men's club, and this together with various mechanical improvements for processing cotton made Reddish a 'model' manufacturing settlement. After which member of the Houldsworth family the public house is named could be a puzzle. It had been thought that it was named after Sir William (below) but as he was a strong supporter of the Church of England Temperance Society it probably was not him they had in mind when naming the public house.

SECTION SEVEN

STOCKPORT THEN & NOW

Mersey Square as it is today. Sometimes it is easy to look at photographs of yesterday and to imagine how it all once looked, especially if there is still a large building there. Sometimes it is a culture shock as everything has been cleared and only the roads remain. So it is with Mersey Square. You can have quite a puzzle comparing the above picture with those of Mersey Square in Section One. Even the name of the road leading away up to St Peter's Way has changed once or twice; it was called St Peter's Square at one time and Rock Row before that.

The town end of Bridge Street leading away from the Market Place. This part of Bridge Street has had a few names over the years, including Briarly's Brow, after the man who once owned the property here. The pub Briarly's on the right started life as the Hole in the Wall (below) said to be named after a large hole (cave) cut into the sandstone at the rear of the hotel. For many years it was the King's Arms and was first mentioned in 1820. The older postcard (below) is a Grenville Series from about 1920.

Prince's Street should always have an apostrophe to remind us it was named after the Prince of Wales. The street today (below) contains the cheaper side of Stockport's shopping; above is the same spot in about 1920. Tram No. 33 has just come in from Reddish. (E. Gray Collection)

The junction of Egerton Street and Lancashire Hill (above), turning left over the motorway and up the hill. It is strange to think that under all those overpasses and junctions is the original Lancashire Bridge. The area on the skyline is a conservation area and very pleasant to walk around. St Mary's Roman Catholic Church spire is on the left and the Christadelphian Church Hall is on the right. Below is a view of Bridge Street as it is today, 1997.

It will take some imagining, but this picture, taken in about 1950, is the same view as that in the bottom picture opposite. The Crown wallpaper shop is now the William Hill betting shop. Lancashire Hill ran straight down into Tiviot Dale and that ran straight into Bridge Street; many old pictures captioned Bridge Street or Tiviot Dale would show more of the other. It was once the main way into the town from the north. People poured in from Tiviot Dale station, trams came in from Reddish, and cars and lorries came that way to get into the town centre. Tiviot Dale ran over Lancashire Bridge, the original bridge at Stockport. This bit of Bridge Street is now a quiet backwater used for parking outside the church and by pedestrians. The Station Hotel, behind the tram, closed in the 1950s and then opened again as Stockport's first gay pub with the wonderful name, Inn with a Chance. However, structural difficulties meant that it had to close again and it was demolished five years later. The haunted Railway Inn next door is still standing and worth a visit for its lovely snug, train pictures and the ghost.

Castle Street, Edgeley. Above, two soldiers take a Sunday afternoon stroll, *c.* 1920. They might have been staying at the Armoury on manoeuvres. Look at the number of pedestrians, even though the cameraman has caught the street with no trams or horse-and-carts. Below is the same street on a Sunday afternoon in April 1997 with hardly a soul about.

The Armoury, on the corner of Greek Street and Shaw Heath. Built in 1862 with a drill ground adjoining it for parades, it was first used by the Volunteer Movement, and the Stockport Volunteers paraded and square-bashed there for many years. Later it was used by the Territorial Force and the TA. The Armoury public house next door was originally a Bell's pub but was taken over by Robinson's in 1949. Recently it has been completely refurbished almost to its original Victorian appearance.

Market Place, Stockport, *c.* 1895. Stockport's two market halls are on the left and right. The colonnaded building (right) is the original market hall, and inside those arches buying and selling went on. Above the arches the business of the town was conducted, proclamations read from the balcony and rates levied. Later it became the post office and then the public library. On the left is the Victorian iron-framed market hall, originally open at street level, which led the *Stockport Advertiser* to dub it 'an umbrella on legs'. The photograph below shows the scene on a quiet Sunday morning today. The old market hall has lost its balcony, but still sports the Stockport coat of arms from 1851. In 1986 the Victorian market hall (to the left of this picture) was saved by a petition signed by over 35,000 people, and restored at a cost of £550,000.

Here is another modern picture to compare with pictures earlier in the book, showing the new entrance to the now-famous Stockport Caves. These caves are man-made, and were used as air-raid shelters during the Second World War. There is a story that a barber called Jackie Lomas kept two bears in a cave on Chestergate at the bottom of Low Bankside (later called Pickford's Brow) where the cave entrance is now. Some stories tell of how the bears were used to advertise the jars of bear grease that he sold for keeping hair in place. Some tell of the bears' being bated with dogs in Mersey Square, and one tale even says the bear (a Catamount bear) could 'cut hair as well as any Christian'. It would have taken more than Mr Lomas' brylcreem to keep me in place if a barbarous bear with a pair of scissors approached.

There are still caves along the River Mersey lower down, which were made into small storerooms by some shopkeepers in Chestergate. An inn demolished during the road-widening scheme of the mid-1930s had a wine and beer cellar cut into the sandstone there.

Little Underbank as it is today, roadworks and all. Compare these pictures with those of the area earlier in the book. The pubs have changed little over the years. There was one called the Black Boy facing the White Lion, and it was here that Stockport's first Sunday School was held. It was demolished in 1823 to give more room for the mail coaches pulling away from the White Lion. There was a pub on Little Underbank in the 1820s called Labour in Vain and on its sign was a lady with a small black boy in a tub, trying to scrub him white! There is no trace of the pub today, and that sign would certainly not be allowed these days. Another pub, the Turners Vaults (now the Queen's Head), just before the bridge, started life as the Queen Anne, first mentioned in 1790. It also had its own distillery, when it was owned by the Turner family in the late eighteenth century.

Winter's restaurant and café. The original clockmaker's and jeweller's shop was always been a focal point with its clock and those lovely carved figures, which are 100 years old. They can be seen quite clearly from the Petersgate Bridge.

Hollywood may be the film capital of America, but it is also the name of an area of Stockport. This is a view of Hollywood Park looking towards the viaduct just before the First World War.

The same view as above, 1997. Although the viaduct has not changed, and the park area is still there, the chimneys, which were a symbol of Stockport's industry, have long gone. There are more than fifteen chimneys in the earlier postcard and not one in the present-day picture.

Castle Street, Edgeley, *c.* 1907. The postcard above shows the electric tram wires and tramlines laid among the setts. William Deacon's Bank stands on the right, but is the grocer's shop on the left now the site of the Grapes Hotel? Below is the present-day view of Castle Street, with its pedestrianized area. The street name reflects the fact that Stockport did once have a castle (near Market Square). The Grapes Hotel on the left is well known for its large collection of teapots above the bar. One of the old tall chimney stacks is still discernible on the right.

The Staircase Café is part of Stockport's proud history. Unfortunately, it is a part that was almost lost to us recently in the Shawcross Fold Redevelopment (Shawcross Fold is the area behind Staircase House). At the last minute a rescue plan was proposed. Stockport Council, English Heritage and the private owners have together formed their own 'Millennium Project' and seem well on the way to saving this building.

The Staircase Café as it is today, undergoing restoration. It is Stockport's oldest building and shown on a map from 1680. It is believed to have been owned by William Dodge, Mayor of Stockport in 1483. The Staircase itself dates from the 1600s and is probably one of the finest examples surviving from that era. It is said that one of Bonny Prince Charlie's commanders, Lord Elcho, stayed there. I wonder if the ghosts will stay after the restoration. Some say there are upward of three ghosts in this building.

The Market Place, *c*. 1910. The parish church dominates the scene, which also shows the Staircase Café with its brick façade. The Staircase building is really in three sections, with the three-storey Staircase Café in the middle. The stairway was rediscovered in 1955 and once it was uncovered ghosts and psychic disturbances started to make their presence felt. Knocking, strange sounds, and tapping nearly drove the café owner Miss Enid Millward crazy. However, she was a brave soul. 'The ghost and I will get on just fine,' she told a *Stockport Advertiser* reporter.

The White Lion on Underbank, one of Stockport's historic pubs. Today it has to fight for trade with its more modern counterparts and has a 'Live Gigs' poster outside, to draw in the customers. The original hotel was built in 1743 and can be seen the above view of 1900. The White Lion of today was built in 1904. It was the main coaching house in Stockport. The London Mails and the Cross-Pennine Coaches would make their first or last stop here on their journeys to and from Manchester. It was a very busy hostelry, and a place where you could get all the news. There was even a tradition of firing a cannon to attract attention when important news came in from London.

Prince's Street, formerly Heaton Lane, is in fact on the north side (Lancashire side) of the River Mersey and was renamed when the Prince of Wales visited Stockport to open the new town hall in 1908. Above is a picture taken just after the Second World War, when the trams terminated there. Below is the same scene today.

Underbank Hall, Stockport. The top postcard dates from about 1910 when the building was home to the Manchester & Liverpool District Bank and was their first outlet. This is why the coat of arms of the city of Liverpool is among the stained glass windows inside the bank. The picture below was taken on Easter Monday 1997. Underbank Hall was built in about 1500, as the town house of the Arderne (Arden) family, who were said to be related to William Shakespeare. It was purchased from Lord Alvanley by the banking company, Christy, Lloyd, Winterbottom & Worsley, in 1824 and it has been a bank ever since.

Looking south from Mersey Square towards Wellington Road South. Once called New Road, it was named after the Duke of Wellington in 1827 to commemorate his triumph at Waterloo. Above is the view in the 1930s with the Carlton cinema (later the Essoldo) on the left. It could seat 1,750 people. Below, the scene today; the town hall tower can be seen clearly in the centre.

Some rivers rise, some start from lakes or reservoirs, but the River Mersey does neither of these. Some books say the Mersey rises in the Pennines and some say in the moors, but both are wrong. It starts where the Rivers Goyt and Tame join in Portwood, Stockport. The River Goyt is on the right, flowing in from Vernon Park, and on the left, having just passed under the M63, is the River Tame. It is unusual for rivers to meet and for both names to disappear. This unique spot has been built over and is hidden away. Above is a picture of the spot where the waters are first called the River Mersey. Mersey of course means boundary, and was first applied to this waterway at Liverpool, up to Warrington. The River Tame once continued from this spot down to Warrington, but time has pushed the name Mersey further east until now maps show that the Mersey starts here.

A clearer picture of the confluence of the River Tame and the River Goyt. The M63 motorway runs over the River Tame. Although the building over of the River Mersey in Stockport gave the town more shopping room, it also took away the pleasure of hearing and seeing the water running through the town.

The River Mersey still runs peacefully under and through Stockport. Cross Wellington Road South and into the bus station and there on the right is the River Mersey, quietly flowing down to the Irish Sea. It still rises quickly after a downpour of rain, and in winter months can be seen rushing under Wellington Road Bridge, reminding us of the 'boundary' that caused problems for Prince Rupert in the Civil War, and gave Bonnie Prince Charlie so much trouble in 1745.

Stockport FC, 1996–7. Stockport has never before been in the First Division, but it is now. It may not be history now but it will be one day, and this is the team that won promotion. (*Stockport Express & Advertiser*)

Sunday 4 May 1997 was a day of celebration in Stockport, when the team won automatic promotion to the First Division. Starting at Edgeley Park Ground they paraded through cheering crowds to the town hall, and here Mike Flynn, the captain, acknowledges the thousands of supporters who turned out in terrible weather to honour this momentous achievement for Stockport. (*Stockport Express & Advertiser*)

BRITAIN IN OLD PHOTOGRAPHS

rystwyth & North Ceredigion
nd Abingdon
on
rney: A Second Selection
g the Avon from Stratford to
wkesbury
incham
rsham
nd Amesbury
esey
old & Bestwood
old & Bestwood: A Second
ection
del & the Arun Valley
ourne
nd Ashby-de-la-Zouch
Aircraft
sbury
am & Tooting
uryshire
es, Mortlake & Sheen
sley
onsfield
ord
ordshire at Work
orth
rley
y
ord
n
ingham Railways
p's Stortford &
bridgeworth
pstone & Seaford
pstone & Seaford: A Second
ction
Country Aviation
Country Railways
Country Road Transport
burn
pool
nd Blandford Forum
ley
n
emouth
ord
ree & Bocking at Work
n
wood
water & the River Parrett
ngton
ort & the Bride Valley
ey Hill
on & Hove
on & Hove: A Second
ction
d Bristol
n & Norwood
Broadstairs & St Peters
ey, Keston & Hayes

Buckingham & District
Burford
Bury
Bushbury
Camberwell
Cambridge
Cannock Yesterday & Today
Canterbury: A Second Selection
Castle Combe to Malmesbury
Chadwell Heath
Chard & Ilminster
Chatham Dockyard
Chatham & Gillingham
Cheadle
Cheam & Belmont
Chelmsford
Cheltenham: A Second Selection
Cheltenham at War
Cheltenham in the 1950s
Chepstow & the River Wye
Chesham Yesterday & Today
Cheshire Railways
Chester
Chippenham & Lacock
Chiswick
Chorley & District
Cirencester
Around Cirencester
Clacton-on-Sea
Around Clitheroe
Clwyd Railways
Clydesdale
Colchester
Colchester 1940–70
Colyton & Seaton
The Cornish Coast
Corsham & Box
The North Cotswolds
Coventry: A Second Selection
Around Coventry
Cowes & East Cowes
Crawley New Town
Around Crawley
Crewkerne & the Ham Stone
Villages
Cromer
Croydon
Crystal Palace, Penge & Anerley
Darlington
Darlington: A Second Selection
Dawlish & Teignmouth
Deal
Derby
Around Devizes
Devon Aerodromes
East Devon at War
Around Didcot & the Hagbournes
Dorchester
Douglas
Dumfries
Dundee at Work
Durham People

Durham at Work
Ealing & Northfields
East Grinstead
East Ham
Eastbourne
Elgin
Eltham
Ely
Enfield
Around Epsom
Esher
Evesham to Bredon
Exeter
Exmouth & Budleigh Salterton
Fairey Aircraft
Falmouth
Farnborough
Farnham: A Second Selection
Fleetwood
Folkestone: A Second Selection
Folkestone: A Third Selection
The Forest of Dean
Frome
Fulham
Galashiels
Garsington
Around Garstang
Around Gillingham
Gloucester
Gloucester: from the Walwin
Collection
North Gloucestershire at War
South Gloucestershire at War
Gosport
Goudhurst to Tenterden
Grantham
Gravesend
Around Gravesham
Around Grays
Great Yarmouth
Great Yarmouth: A Second
Selection
Greenwich & Woolwich
Grimsby
Around Grimsby
Grimsby Docks
Gwynedd Railways
Hackney: A Second Selection
Hackney: A Third Selection
From Haldon to Mid-Dartmoor
Hammersmith & Shepherds Bush
Hampstead to Primrose Hill
Harrow & Pinner
Hastings
Hastings: A Second Selection
Haverfordwest
Hayes & West Drayton
Around Haywards Heath
Around Heathfield
Around Heathfield: A Second
Selection
Around Helston

Around Henley-on-Thames
Herefordshire
Herne Bay
Heywood
The High Weald
The High Weald: A Second
Selection
Around Highworth
Around Highworth & Faringdon
Hitchin
Holderness
Honiton & the Otter Valley
Horsham & District
Houghton-le-Spring &
Hetton-le-Hole
Houghton-le-Spring & Hetton-le-
Hole: A Second Selection
Huddersfield: A Second Selection
Huddersfield: A Third Selection
Ilford
Ilfracombe
Ipswich: A Second Selection
Islington
Jersey: A Third Selection
Kendal
Kensington & Chelsea
East Kent at War
Keswick & the Central Lakes
Around Keynsham & Saltford
The Changing Face of Keynsham
Kingsbridge
Kingston
Kinver
Kirkby & District
Kirkby Lonsdale
Around Kirkham
Knowle & Dorridge
The Lake Counties at Work
Lancashire
The Lancashire Coast
Lancashire North of the Sands
Lancashire Railways
East Lancashire at War
Around Lancaster
Lancing & Sompting
Around Leamington Spa
Around Leamington Spa:
A Second Selection
Leeds in the News
Leeds Road & Rail
Around Leek
Leicester
The Changing Face of Leicester
Leicester at Work
Leicestershire People
Around Leighton Buzzard &
Linslade
Letchworth
Lewes
Lewisham & Deptford:
A Second Selection
Lichfield